BACH and HANDEL

The Consummation of the Baroque in Music

ARCHIBALD T. DAVISON

HARVARD UNIVERSITY PRESS

CAMBRIDGE · MASSACHUSETTS

1951

THIS BOOK IS BASED ON LECTURES
DELIVERED AT THE UNIVERSITY OF
VIRGINIA UNDER THE PAGE-BARBOUR
FOUNDATION ON APRIL 3, 4, AND 5,
1950

Foreword

Almost every year since the establishment of the Page-Barbour Foundation in 1907 the course of lectures delivered under its auspices has appeared in book form. The volume of 1950 probably contains less visible substance than any of its predecessors owing to the fact that some time out of each evening was devoted to those music illustrations which will be found listed at the end of this book. The music, by far the most significant part of the lectures, not only furnished pleasure and enlightenment to the audience but was, as well, a reinforcement to one acutely conscious of the honor of standing in such a distinguished succession of speakers, and who was, besides, charged with the responsibility of interpreting two composers whose distinction has seldom been equaled. There was comfort in the realization that from time to time the lecturer might find refuge behind the towering figures of Bach and Handel and allow his voice to be lost in the real and convincing eloquence of their music.

Gratitude is here expressed to the players and singers for the performance of the illustrations and to Professor Stephen D. Tuttle of the University of Virginia whose painstaking and artistic direction would certainly have satisfied even the exacting standards of J. S. B. and G. F. H.

Thanks are due to the following for permission to include excerpts from their publications: the Oxford University Press; the Clarendon Press; W. W. Norton & Co.; A. & C. Black, Ltd.; the Macmillan Co.; G. P. Putnam's Sons; the Unicorn Press; and the Harvard University Press.

ARCHIBALD T. DAVISON

Cambridge, Massachusetts
January 1, 1951

BACH and HANDEL

The Consummation of
the Baroque in Music

I

The year 1950, the two-hundredth anniversary of the death of John Sebastian Bach, was a year full of significance for music and an occasion for the celebration of the greatness of one whose contributions rank with the foremost in any sphere of art. The lectures which make up this small book might well have been devoted exclusively to Bach, but without a consideration of Handel the story of the baroque or thorough-bass period could be but partially told. The achievements of these two men were in many respects different, and the paths by which they gained them were not always the same, but it is together, and not singly, that they represent the consummation of their age. As composers, their procedure is a compound of many features, some of them easy to identify, others susceptible only of speculation. The sources upon which Handel drew are sometimes quite obvious, but the well of Bach's inspiration is by no means easily accessible. Certainly both owed some debt to the past, and I think it may be profitable to look backward—even if for the moment that view embraces only those changes which marked the establishment of the period with which they were associated—and to speak briefly and with necessary omissions of the composers and the evolution of styles and forms within this period up to the point at which our two principals come upon the stage.

The closing years of the sixteenth century were laden with prophecy for the art of music. Certain Renaissance ideals had been fully realized and new ones were pressing their claims. Among the most important of these was the ideal of converting music to dramatic uses. The combining of music and drama had been common from the Middle Ages on, but in the late Renaissance the idea was given impetus partly by a preoccupation with the classics and partly by changes in methods of composition and performance. There were madrigal comedies and other semidramatic types, and there were devices such as the repeated note employed for the emphasis of some salient idea in the text, a usage common in both sacred and secular style and later much exploited in dramatic music of every type. The trend was clearly toward opera, and in the year 1600, in Italy, the birthplace of many of the most significant baroque musical undertakings, the first operas whose music we possess came into being. In the beginning, the movement laid stress on simplicity; it patterned itself on the austerity of the Greek drama, the principles of which composers wished to parallel in their operas. Although the form was humanized and glorified early in the seventeenth century by Monteverdi, Italian opera began, before long, to court those two features which have come generally to be associated with it, namely, melody for its own sake and vocal virtuosity. Italy soon became the virtual ruler of the operatic world, though the works of composers such as Keiser in Germany, Purcell in England, and Lully and Rameau in

2

France did represent a truly native effort as distinguished from both foreign importation and the type of domestic opera which deliberately submitted itself to the influence of foreign style. The typical baroque Italian opera, emphasizing every aspect of the singer's art and cast in an almost invariable form, was extremely popular, and Handel found much in it upon which to model his operatic style.

The oratorio (having passed through its initial stages) was established as a form by Carissimi around the middle years of the seventeenth century. It differed from opera mainly in its adoption of a sacred subject and in its emphasis on the chorus as a distinguishing feature. From Carissimi through Legrenzi, Stradella, and Alessandro Scarlatti the oratorio leads directly to Handel. Within the field of the oratorio falls also the Passion, a subject especially appealing to German composers.

The madrigal, chief secular choral form of the Renaissance, did not survive the rising tide of interest in dramatic music, and with other brief secular types gave way to the cantata, a work generally dramatic in character but without the resources of stage production. It was a solo form with instrumental accompaniment, cultivated everywhere and treated with especial distinction by the Italians. That was the secular cantata, but quite as important for our purposes is a consideration of the church cantata as it is found in the works of German Protestant composers. These cantatas, for which there was an ordained place in the service, were based on some theological concept, often of a general nature, and included solos, choruses, and instrumental accompaniment. A chorale frequently served as the animating core of the work and appeared at intervals either as a whole or in part. Splendid examples are to be found in the work of Pachelbel, Kuhnau, and particularly Buxtehude and Tunder, whose cantatas Bach, in the beginning, probably took as his models.

The word "solo" as applied to vocal music has thus far figured so prominently that I should like to say something of its rise and of its appropriateness to the musical purposes of the baroque period. In the sixteenth century the solo voice was primarily a lyric agent as one discovers it in the "ayres" of Dowland and Campion and in the lute songs of the Spanish composer Milan. In the baroque, conforming to the prevailing spirit of the time, it became the means, and the only fully adequate means, of expressing profound personal feeling. Choral counterpoint, one of the outstanding achievements of the Renaissance, had proved ideal for the conveyance of corporate emotion as a background for those aspects of religious feeling such as awe, adoration, or humility which could be expressed by *groups* of persons. Counterpoint, however, could not vividly portray such sentiments as secular love, hate, or fear; its success in dealing with secular matters was confined to those of an objective kind, to texts about nature, or to personal emotions to which its application might be general rather than individual. In Italy, at the beginning of the baroque period, the monody, chief representative of the "New Music," occupied the attention of composers and became the adopted form of solo expression and the prophet of the later dramatic recitative. The inevitable identification of the single voice as separate from the whole represented a gradual process spread over a considerable part of music history, but the baroque conception of the function of the solo voice is accurately prefigured in the Italian late sixteenth-century practice of performing madrigals with the upper part sung as a solo, the remaining voices supplied by instruments. The true destiny of melody in the Italian baroque, however,

4

rested with the operatic arias of Neapolitan composers like Provenzale and Alessandro Scarlatti; melody which allowed the composer to display his art—and the singer's as well—in demonstrations of vocal virtuosity or in the bel canto with its long, flowing, superlatively vocal line.

If the Renaissance idea of the solo song was unsuited to baroque musical speech, so too was the idea of Renaissance counterpoint, not only because of its limitations in the expression of the personal and dramatic, as has been said, but also because the admission into the musical score of the figured bass had brought about a drastic change in contrapuntal method resulting in a style entirely appropriate to baroque ideals. The pure a cappella style, represented most familiarly by the music of Palestrina, Lassus, and Byrd, had slowly disappeared, to be replaced by a contrapuntal style more harmonically controlled and perfectly adapted to the dramatic

monically controlled and perfectly adapted to the dramatic tendencies of the time. The outer voices the most important, and once the neces- melodic interest among the parts—as had teenth-century counterpoint—had lapsed, o develop a recognizable melodic physiog- , sometimes cast in a repeated pattern or s the melodic stimulus to the invention of stance above it. The Renaissance type of lt of voice leading, became in the baroque posed and more characterizing, and when preparation, in the manner of Monte- immeasurably to the poignancy of the

with these matters was the advent of ple certainly present in the music of the Renaissance but there generally subservient to the demands of counterpoint. In the baroque era harmony became a self-sufficient detail, most useful in pointing up situations in which personal feeling must be tellingly expressed, and a weapon admirably suited to the highlighting of dramatic episodes. The presence of real harmony is attested by the use of thorough bass or the basso continuo, which by means of figures under the bass notes made clear exactly what chords were to be used. Counterpoint was profoundly affected by the use of this feature which definitely circumscribed the contrapuntal flow; and rhythm, especially when applied to vocal music, surrendered the fluid character it had derived from verbal accentuation in the early period and, becoming strictly metered, confined the music within the strait jacket of the measure.

The major interest of the Renaissance in choral music shifted, in the baroque, to instrumental writing, and this was ministered to by the growing physical competance of the instruments themselves. Germany was devoted to the organ, with especial distinction belonging to Protestant composers whose chorale preludes display a steadily mounting achievement both in technique and in expression. Save for the organ music of Frescobaldi, the Italian product hardly parallels the German in excellence. It was the German tradition of elaboration of the church hymns laid down in the early years of the baroque by Scheidt, and almost fulfilled near its close in the work of Buxtehude, that was to lead directly to the transcendent chorale preludes of Bach. Music for keyboard instruments other than the organ reveals, in some cases, characteristically national styles with a maturing sense of the idiomatic qualities of the instruments. The work of François Couperin in France, for whom Bach seems to have had a particularly high regard; of Kuhnau, J. C. F. Fischer, and Gottlieb Muffat in Germany; of Blow and Purcell in

England; and of Domenico Scarlatti in Italy greatly enriched keyboard music and prepared the way for or supplemented the work of Bach and Handel. The modern string family having replaced the older and less manageable viols, an entirely new vista was opened up. All instrumental music had once owed something to vocal style, but once composers had discovered that the violin, for example, was capable of an individual style, violin writing became, in its essentials, what it is today. Evidences of a growing comprehension of the virtuoso and expressive possibilities of the violin are evident in the work of Marini, Porpora, Corelli, and Vitali. It is no accident that in composition for the voice and for strings, united by the common possession of the element of vocality, the Italians should have stood before all others. They were outstanding, also, in chamber and orchestral music in which the strings are all important, and to the strings could be added trumpets, woodwind, and horns. Perhaps the most notable examples of Italian concerted writing are the works of Vivaldi, from which Bach doubtless learned much of value both with regard to the concerto form and the technique of string writing. The principle of concerted instrumental music was exemplified in the trio sonata, in the chamber music of Couperin, and in the concertos of Torelli, Corelli, and Vivaldi, leading to the full realization of the idea in the concerti grossi of Bach and Handel.

In preparing the ground for a consideration of Bach and Handel, the music which came before them is, of course, of great importance, but hardly less significant are the forms in which that music was cast. Many of the older types like the Mass, the motet, and the Passion persisted into the baroque, as well as such instrumental forms as the toccata, the ricercar, and the various dance pieces, and new ones, many of them, to be sure, having their roots in the Renaissance, appeared: the suite, the sonata (so transformed as to be really new), the chorale prelude, and the fugue—the suite, a formal categorical grouping of dances which previously had been somewhat loosely assembled; and the sonata, originally a piece to be played in contrast to something sung, later allied with the suite and eventually taking on formal and stylistic properties of its own. So it was with the other forms, all of them evolutionary, some of them realizing their full possibilities in the baroque period, some of them proceeding to a larger destiny in the ages which followed.

Besides formal extension there are questions affecting the integrity of the music as a whole—its continuity and the development of the ideas upon which it is based. Take the fugue, so prominent in the works of Bach and Handel, as an example. Like so many of the forms of the sixteenth century, its basis is contrapuntal imitation, but even with the constantly increasing skill in handling this device, to say nothing of the opportunity for the more effective employment of it offered by the tonal system, there were certain structural considerations which had to be met before the fugue could attain its full stature as an art form. In particular, the problems of continuity and development in its elementary sense had to be solved. It is only necessary to examine the capriccios and fugues of Bach's predecessors—even the fugues of Buxtehude who came just before him—to observe the frequently periodic nature of the movement, the occasional absence of smooth articulation, and the neglect of the developmental potentialities of the material. The single theme of a fugue offered limited possibilities for expansion, and unless subjected to the workings of a propulsive kind of musical imagination, the episodes, which constitute the main body of the movement, were bound to be truncated. Structural continuity and the development of the musical idea are germane to all musical forms, but nowhere are they more crucial than in the fugue.

Here, then, are at least some of the chief ingredients which came ready to the hand of Bach and Handel: an age that was markedly Italianate; an opera which, with a few distinguished exceptions, was dominated by the Italian method; a variety of vocal forms including the oratorio, the Passion, and the cantata; and a well-developed instrumental style in all its branches. Had these two composers never lived, the music of the baroque era up to their time would doubtless seem to us an artistic product complete in itself, but its full capacities are revealed only in the light of their contributions to it; to the forms in which it was cast; to the musical language in which it was written. This makes the greatness of composers like Buxtehude, Keiser, and the Scarlattis appear to be only relative, and although this is manifestly unjust, it is nonetheless undeniable.

Earlier I mentioned the fact that Bach and Handel, though they were contemporaries whose work covers to a great extent common ground, were in many respects quite different. Actually, the linking of the two is not warranted by the facts of music history. We do so link them because they lived at the same time, and because together they constitute the crowning glory of a great period. Certainly the contemporaries of Bach and Handel saw them as quite different musical personalities. "Solid old fellows like Forkel," as Ernest Newman says, "who had the capacity to perceive what is eternal in the seemingly old-fashioned procedures of Bach, plumping for him as against Händel; while the Bright Young People of the epoch, who prided themselves, as the Bright Young

9

People always do, on being terrifically up-to-date, preferred Händel because of his franker appeal to the dominant musical mentality of that day."[1] In the nineteenth century, as Newman later points out, Bach was the favorite of the Romantics because his musical speech had more in common with their ideals and Handel seemed like a figure belonging to another era. Both were skillful contrapuntists and orchestrators, and as artists they shared the common heritage of eighteenth-century musical language, but they spoke it with a different accent and often with different ends in view. As individuals, both were born in the same year, and in later life both went blind; and this, roughly, is the sum of their likenesses one to the other. It is generally believed that in spite of Bach's eager attempts to make the acquaintance of Handel, they never met. Unlike the case of those other famous contemporaries, Mozart and Haydn, the influence of the music of Bach on that of Handel and vice versa may only be surmised. As their mentalities and their aesthetic viewpoints were unlike, so each approached music from a fundamentally different angle. Instruments and their particular expressiveness permeated Bach's musical thinking, while through almost all of Handel's music, like Wagner's, shines the poetry of words even when no words are present.

Bach's life centered about the church; Handel's interest was mainly in opera, the oratorio being a medium to which he turned after failure in his chosen field. This does not mean that dramatic expression is absent from Bach's music—far, far from it; and upon this point I mean to dwell later on. When we place Handel's romantic career beside Bach's, the latter's existence seems strikingly uneventful. He had no experience of foreign study or travel as Schütz, the greatest of his German predecessors in the field of Protestant church music had, or Handel, who was a thoroughgoing and highly absorptive cosmopolitan. Bach's career is an almost unbroken record of work; of the continuous composition of masterpieces. Nor am I forgetting that extra-musical manifestation of his creative power, a feat that inspires me with an awe comparable to that which I feel for his music, namely, his fathering of twenty children. During his lifetime he received no such acclaim as did Handel or his Italian contemporaries, and within a few years after his death his star had set apparently not to rise again. Knowledge of his greatness rested only with the few of his associates who survived him, and any mention of the name "Bach" in the latter half of the eighteenth century would have been taken as referring to any of the older Bach's gifted sons. One of them, Karl Philipp Emanuel, speaking of composers of canons, went so far as to utter a direct indictment of his father's contrapuntal wizardry as it is manifested in his music by the statement that "it was ever a certain proof of a total want of genius in any one that was fond of such wretched studies and unmeaning productions." [2] Applicable to this, certainly, is the comment of Bliss Perry concerning the critics of a great citizen of Boston, that they were "confidently wrong." Bach's *Passion According to St. Matthew* was practically unheard until Mendelssohn revived it in a performance of 1829, its place having been taken by *Der Tod Jesu* by Karl Heinrich Graun, a Passion which pays obvious tribute to the prevailing Italian style and which is now seldom mentioned save to emphasize the miracle of Bach's musical resurrection.

The work of Bach and Handel may be compared at many points; but perhaps the most exact field of comparison is that of their choral compositions; not only because each was in his own way there supreme, but also because the choral music of both, granting internal differences, springs like all choral music not from abstract musical ideas but from those which derive their authority from words. Save under exceptional circumstances, performances of Bach's greater choral works are somewhat unusual, being generally confided to a chorus of skilled singers. So it is that they are not familiar to most of us, either through singing them or hearing them. Handel, on the other hand, is well known to us through his *Messiah*, which, to the almost total exclusion of his other magnificent oratorios, has become as universal a possession as our membership in the human race. Years ago, when I read the statement that a missionary had heard the well-known motif of the "Hallelujah Chorus" sung by savages in darkest Africa, it seemed to me the essence of the fantastic. Today my skepticism is considerably abated. *Messiah* is apparently ubiquitous. It vies with the plum pudding as a constant in English life; and in this country, having ceased to be the exclusive property of the solid, veteran, middle-aged chorus, it has been passed over to the ministrations of assorted community musical groups, and to the service of music education, under whose auspices it is annually and enthusiastically piped by hosts of little children from the halls of a thousand public schools. *Messiah*, then, is our nearest musical relative, and by far the most intelligible illustration to be found of Handel's way with a chorus.

Both Bach and Handel were skilled contrapuntists, but Handel's counterpoint is, like the typical counterpoint of the thorough-bass period, strongly dependent on harmony as a structural reinforcement. The harmonic pillars which run up through his polyphony are more clearly heard and more regular in their incidence than is the case with Bach, whose counterpoint, while it recognizes the inevitable presence of harmony, employs it more as an adjunct and less as a full partner than is the case with Handel. In this particular Bach's affiliations are with the era when each line of the counterpoint was to a great extent its own master. Handel often seems to be forecasting the method of the composers of the "gallant style" who wrote in the period following the baroque, and whose music frequently suggests harmonic decoration rather than true counterpoint.

In the generation preceding that of Bach, and in Bach's own time, a sense of vocality, of the true vocal line, and of a feeling for what is idiomatically choral had disappeared from German Protestant sacred writing, and instrumental thinking dominated the entire process. Handel was not affected by this because he had assimilated the native Italian vocal sense and had added to it what he had learned of the secret of English choral art, chiefly through the works of Purcell. One aspect of Bach's preoccupation with instrumental style is shown by his fondness for transferring to the choral field, especially in the cantatas, the structural outlines of one or another of the forms in which he cast his chorale preludes, and under these circumstances we sometimes wish that he had given a little more elbow room to his text instead of restraining it within the confines of a predetermined form. Handel was too much concerned with the words to allow formal considerations to affect him. One has only to recall the chorus "All We Like Sheep Have Gone Astray" from *Messiah*, in which Handel cannot bring himself to pursue relentlessly to the end the none too significant music he had borrowed from his secular Italian duets but changes suddenly at the close to newly composed and inspired music for the words "and the Lord hath laid on him the iniquity of us all." This completely upsets the form, but it is at once a witness to Handel's artistic probity and to his genius as a composer. No more dramatic contrast between the methods of the two in dealing with a text could be offered than their respective settings of "Glory to God in the Highest," Handel in *Messiah*, Bach in the *Christmas Oratorio:* Handel's very human-sounding angels singing their praise mainly in simple, exuberant outbursts of harmony, and at the end making their exit right and left to a brief and inescapably ballet-like postlude; Bach, immersed in contrapuntal abstraction, writing a chorus of transcendent power but so complex and so crowded with difficulties that had it fallen to the lot of the celestial choir to sing it in celebration of the nativity, one may feel sure that even for that expert body any number of extra rehearsals would have been required.

Bach was concerned with musical *ideas,* and it sometimes seems as though it made small difference to him through what medium he expressed them. I remember that some years ago in Edinburgh the late Donald Tovey told me that as an experiment he had partially rescored two or three pieces of Bach, because from considerations of range and technique he was convinced that Bach, while composing, had, in the back of his mind, instruments other than those he actually employed. In the same way it is not difficult to believe that in more than one vocal instance it was instruments and not voices that were sounding in the ear of Bach's mind. Indeed, if Bach did not think of voices as instruments, he frequently wrote as though he did, with a resulting disregard for the limitations of the vocal mechanism. Someone has pointed out that in Cantata 180 Bach asks the soprano to sing twenty-four measures without any rest; and elsewhere the tenor is required to sing thirty-five measures with only four measures of rest. Bach's treatment of the tenor was, on occasions, certainly not humane, and we sometimes come to view that voice with the distaste we feel for the oboe in the accompaniments of Brahms's choral works. What many must have felt has been admirably expressed by Fuller Maitland in this way: "It must be owned," he says, "that in the cantatas there are not a few numbers which seem as if Bach had a special detestation of the tenor voice as well as a low opinion of the intellectual capacity that generally accompanies it." [3]

Choral singers who dote on the vocal line of least resistance often resent what appears to be Bach's indifference to natural procedure, simply because they either cannot or will not cope with the unexpected. Handel is vocality incarnate. He not only knew what the public wanted, but he was as well an infallible judge of what the singer loves to do. Take as an example his decorative choral passages; once Handel sets the pattern he generally preserves it. You may be a measure or two late in turning the page, but when you get there you are not likely to find that he has altered the formula. But it is never safe to try to anticipate Bach. In the expression of his ideas he was forever varying the detail, often for harmonic reasons, and the singer who, glancing up the slope of a long and provocative Bachian roulade, closes his eyes, teeters back and forth from heel to toe, and proceeds to let vocal nature take its course is likely to be brought up with a short turn. However, Bach never sets a vocal problem which the singers with the aid of the conductor cannot solve. Many a singer is unable to achieve in a single breath one of those long, exciting, coloratura passages, to say nothing of increasing the volume as he proceeds; yet if he is told not to go as far as he can in a single breath, but to take quick and fairly full ones early and often, the result may be a climax of overwhelming brilliance. Does a part find itself com-

15

mitted to make a fugal entrance in a range where it is hopelessly buried by the other voices? Then the conductor has only to reinforce that entrance by singers borrowed from another part. These are simple matters, and a conductor who would deal honestly with Bach's choral music must have regard for them. Bach's storming of the choral heights is not like that of Beethoven, who tries the voices almost beyond endurance by keeping them at the top of their range for long periods. The physical demands which Bach makes of the singer are different—Beethoven demoralizes the vocal mechanism; Bach lays an equal tax on brains and lungs; and Handel, incidentally, never does either.

Hugo Leichtentritt has written of the care with which Handel, having in mind the particular character of a key, chose for example the appropriate tonality for each of his opera arias.[4] How far Handel observed the affective nature of the different keys in setting his choruses I cannot say, but Handel being Handel, I suspect that his choice was dictated mainly by choral considerations. In any case, the diversity of keys is notably larger in *Messiah* than it is in either the *B minor Mass* or the *Magnificat*. Bach first wrote the *Magnificat* in E flat but later scored it in D, and here, quite possibly, an instrumental consideration entered into the calculation. Bach frequently employed the trumpet in D, the natural resources of that instrument ministering admirably to effects of a joyous, triumphant, or ceremonial kind, and with these trumpets went also the tympani, tuned in D when Bach elected to use them.[5] Whatever principle may have guided these composers in their key selection, neither one felt, as far as I have observed, any restraint in their choice, but the key of D suited them both—Bach perhaps more consistently than Handel—when brilliance and high sonority were desired. In *Messiah*,

16

D is the tonality for six of the twenty-one choruses; but in Bach's *B minor Mass* the proportion is greater, being nine out of fifteen; and in the *Magnificat*, of the five choruses, four are in D. The *B minor Mass* was composed in 1733 and with the *Magnificat*, written ten years earlier, contains pages which exhibit Bach at the apex of his brilliance as a choral composer. No greater tribute could be offered than to say that in these works Bach approaches most nearly the choral power of Handel.

Handel's choral texture is likely to be more of the open-work variety than is Bach's. The latter often exceeds the customary four parts for the single chorus and uses the double-chorus medium as well, while Handel seldom departs from the four-voice scheme. For this reason, in part at least, Handel's choral scores are less complex and seem less crowded than do Bach's. But the basic difference in effect results, I believe, from the fact that Handel, through orchestra and chorus combined, achieves sonority on two planes, while Bach's orchestra tends to merge with the chorus to create a single mass of sound. Thus, Handel's choral writing is self-sufficient. Bach, on the other hand, is generally concerned with the single vocal line, and if its destiny decrees that it shall lie in an ineffective part of the range when a fortissimo is in the making, the orchestra is there to fill out the texture, and it is the singer and not the listener who experiences disappointment. By a simple device which does not particularly impress the eye but which works aural magic, namely, the grouping of the men's voices in a high register and the women's voices sometimes in a relatively low one, Handel was able to achieve choral effects of great sonority and intensity. We are accustomed to associate this method with brief dramatic ejaculations, but Handel could also employ it more subtly to create a tension arising from the pathetic nature of the text. Although Bach uses it with striking effect in the chorus "I Would Beside My Lord" from the *Passion According to St. Matthew,* the true vocal inwardness of the device was known primarily to Handel.

As a choral architect, Handel was no match for his great contemporary. Bach's invention is so spontaneous and so unflagging that from the opening bar of a chorus the music seems to progress with irresistible momentum. This results in longer and less sectionalized choruses and in an amazingly varied key scheme. A chorus of Handel's, comparable in length to one of Bach's, is likely to be divided into separate movements, each based on a different musical idea. Both men leaned heavily on text repetition, and with Bach it was a providential device, as it permitted him to develop his musical ideas to whatever extent he chose, using the text as a vehicle for choral participation. Handel, the opera composer, seldom missed an opportunity to introduce into his choruses effective dramatic strokes, a resource which Bach never felt called upon to employ unless it was inevitably appropriate to the textual occasion. One of Handel's most potent devices was the setting up of some sort of energetic scurrying about in the orchestra through which there penetrated mighty hammer blows of harmony struck by the chorus. A familiar example is his treatment of the words "wonderful" and "counsellor" in the chorus "For Unto Us a Child Is Born" from *Messiah.* Bach, I think, found it difficult to interrupt the continuity of his musical thought in this way, but his uses of harmony set in dramatic contrast to counterpoint are the more telling for their infrequency.

Some have wished that Bach had taken a leaf from Handel's choral notebook, particularly at the final cadences of some of his mightier choruses. These malcontents remind me of those who would have Romeo return to consciousness long enough to discover that Juliet had not died when he supposed, but had killed herself in grief over his self-destruction. Bach's greatness is sufficiently overwhelming; it needs no admixture of Handel; and I would suggest that any tightening of the choral climax superimposed on the final measures of the "Et Resurrexit" in the *B minor Mass*, shall we say, would constitute nothing less than a dangerously shattering emotional experience.

The bulk of Bach's choral composition is represented by the cantatas which he wrote for the Protestant service and which cover thirty years of his musical activity. Like the number of his Passions, the number of his cantatas is variously estimated; but there must have been at least three hundred, and of these only about two hundred remain to us. To know even a relatively small part of these works, to perceive the endless variety they embody and the eloquence they contain, is to realize the tragedy of the loss of so many of these cantatas as well as others of the master's works. The librettos of the cantatas were framed about the traditional theological concepts of Protestantism and were attentive to the significance of a particular day or feast of the church year. In addition, Bach composed some twenty-one secular cantatas which reveal a quite different aspect of his genius. To the foregoing works may be added the motets written for the Leipzig services and for special occasions. Then there are the Passions and the *Christmas Oratorio*, actually a set of six separate cantatas unified through their conveyance of the entire story of the birth of Christ; and finally, the monumental *Mass in B minor* which Bach never performed, and the much shorter and deeply impressive *Magnificat*. This does not comprise Bach's total choral output, but it includes the larger part of it.

From this list I have arbitrarily selected three types, each one quite different from the others and each one thoroughly characteristic. They are the motet, the Magnificat, and the Passion.

The German motet of the late baroque was a far different type of composition from that which was cultivated by composers of the sixteenth century, like Palestrina. That was the heyday of pure choral style, and the idea of vocality as it is manifested in the Latin motets of the period had later given place to a more instrumental concept of writing. The transformation is evident in many particulars: in a more abstract vocal line, and in a contrapuntal fabric controlled by the more frequently placed and often regularly recurring struts of harmony. The structure, too, is affected by changed ideals of rhythm and the substitution of the tonal for the modal system of scales which enhanced variety through tonal modulation. The tradition of motet composition persists throughout the history of the Reformed Church to the end of the baroque era, and at Leipzig, certainly, it was an accepted part of the service. One of the issues connected with choral music in the sixteenth century which is still active concerning that of the eighteenth is the question of accompaniment. Where choirs were small or inexpert, or the music measurably difficult, the doubling of the voices with instruments seems entirely probable; but granting changes in attitude toward many features of music in the course of its development, there would appear to be ample evidence that the psychology of singers has never changed from the birth of music as an art. Palestrina and his contemporaries wrote music that is so exclusively vocal in its nature that those of us who have sung and conducted it would be loath to admit that singers of that day, whose very property that music was, would have welcomed instrumental participation save under the circumstances just mentioned. Bach's ideal of choral writing was, indeed, far from that of Palestrina; and it may be that for Bach instruments were an inevitable feature of choral performance—he did, in fact, arrange a Mass of Palestrina with instrumental accompaniment including organ. What may be said, then, of accompaniment for Bach's motets? For one of these, at least, he supplied an accompaniment, and it is, of course, possible that the accompaniments to the others have been lost. In view of the formidable vocal difficulty of some of the motets, and the known slightness of the musical forces on which Bach could depend, the possibility of accompaniment cannot be denied. Schweitzer believes that in the Germany of Bach's time the term "a cappella" meant not unaccompanied singing, but singing with instrumental doubling of the voices and the invariable participation of the organ;[6] but he later suggests that with the highly efficient choruses of our time we perhaps ought to omit accompaniment for the motets. In the end, however, he states it as his conviction that the most effective performance may be gained by a not too large chorus supported by the organ.[7] The matter, then, seems to be left to individual choice, and all that needs to be said is that whether sung accompanied or without instruments, the motets of Bach rank among his greater choral triumphs.

Of all Bach's choral music the motets are the least often performed, owing no doubt to the prodigious difficulties involved in an unaccompanied performance. On those rare occasions when a Bach motet is presented the choice is likely to fall on *Singet dem Herrn,* partly because of its brilliance and partly because it offers a challenge to the virtuoso capacities of any chorus however skilled. Concentration on no more than a few motets at most has led to the neglect of others not less great as music but not so instant in their appeal. Among these is certainly the remarkable work *Komm, Jesu, Komm*. This motet, as Whittaker has indicated, is the only one by Bach for which the text, excluding hymn verses, is not scriptural.[8] It is divided by Bach into three sections, proceeding without a noticeable break. Each of these sections he treats in a different meter, and he closes the final section with a chorale-like movement called an "aria." Those who question Bach's melodic gift should be referred to this aria, which stands among the most expressive and finely constructed of his melodies. Except for the fact that the second section begins with an augmentation of the closing notes of the first section, there is no obvious effort to create unity, and certainly none in behalf of variety. The piece is scored, to be sure, for double chorus, but there is no brilliant antiphony; the choruses simply reinforce one another in their pleading and in their confidence. However, any suspicion of monotony that the eye of the casual reader may harbor is quickly confounded by the ear, for Bach has written himself into this motet: his deep religious feeling, his technique that could make that feeling vivid in every note, and above all his power of expression that endows the work with a poignancy which Bach alone knew how to invoke. There is no evidence regarding the circumstances which prompted Bach to write this motet, but Terry believes that it was composed for a funeral occasion.[9]

Bach wrote two Magnificats of which one, for soprano solo, has been lost. The other was probably written for the Christmas Vespers at Leipzig in 1723. It is the shortest and the earliest of Bach's major choral works and demonstrates, among other things, what the Italian cantata style could be when transfigured by genius. The Italian approach is evident in many particulars: in the harmonic nature of certain of the accompaniments, in the long successions of thirds and sixths, in the unusually gracious vocal writing in the solos, and in its obviously dramatic derivation. The close of the chorus "Fecit potentiam" is not the type of drama in which Bach customarily indulged; it is much more in the manner of Handel and suggests the familiar Handelian cadence, with which that composer was wont to stop the proceedings by a sudden pause, after which would come a few concluding measures in resounding fortissimo.

Bach's own hand, however, is manifest in the symbolism. On this point Parry says, "the word 'Gloria' in the final chorus seems to have inspired him with the idea of the expansion of all-embracing splendor of glory, which he suggests by piling up the voices in superincumbent passages of triplets, from low bass notes upward to the high soprano entry, which completes the mighty final chord—a process which he repeats twice with interesting modifications, so providing for three clauses—that is once for each person of the Trinity." [10] A more obvious case is the "Omnes generationes" in which Bach sees the unbroken stream of marching generations, each one arriving in due course and joining its predecessors in a kind of animated bustling about, until at the end, as though the composer foresaw the eventual overpopulation of the world, he makes the generations crowd up from behind and tread on each other's heels. There are two features of this chorus that particularly interest me: first, it is an entire and a not too brief chorus constructed on a text of two words which constitute the subject of a sentence without a predicate; and it is, of all the vocal music of Bach that I know, the most earthy.[11]

I think it is a mistake to say that this work represents less than the complete Bach simply because it is not written in his profounder style. I cannot imagine any other composer than Bach as its author, for whatever he assimilated from sources outside himself he transfigured with his own particular might. The *Magnificat* is probably Bach's most popular choral work, and it is, as well, a glorious artistic creation.

Just when the text of the Passion story was first accompanied by music it is impossible to say, but in the Middle Ages, at least, it appears to have been sung on different days of Holy Week to a type of plainchant conveying the accounts of the four Evangelists. A priest sang the part of Christ, the narrative sections and the outbursts of the people being performed by others of the clergy. By the sixteenth century choral settings had replaced the simpler music, and these developed into two types, the motet Passion and the dramatic Passion. In the motet form the entire text was set continuously for chorus, while in the dramatic form the Evangelist's account was given to the older Passion Tones which had evolved into melodic formulae from the earlier plainsong use. These formulae, in turn, became transformed into recitative. To the chorus was given music for the actual spoken words as they occur in the story.

With the lapse of interest in the purely vocal types, with the rise of accompaniment and of preoccupation with the opera, the Passion undergoes important changes; true recitative appears, the orchestra is used, and there are solos and chorales. With this characteristic seventeenth-century arrangement, the outward form of the Passion is what it was when Bach set it. The number of his Passions has been estimated at five, but opinion is fairly agreed that only three may with certainty be ascribed to him: the *St. John* in 1723; the *St. Matthew* in 1729; and the *St. Mark*, not now extant, perhaps partly drawn from a funeral ode of 1727.

To state as a fact that Bach's choral music is generally not intrinsically vocal, that it is difficult to learn and to sing, implies not the slightest criticism. Indeed, I consider it one of the fortuitous virtues of Bach's music in general that it does demand self-discipline and long and arduous hours of practice on the part of those who would perform it. Let me make a confession. Singers are naturally eager to master the exteriors, and if this comes too easily, to regard the task as largely accomplished. I have taught one college generation after another to sing the works of Bach, and in rehearsal, when there have been errors, instead of being disturbed by them I have rejoiced in them; and when on notably rare occasions mistakes were not sufficiently numerous, I have invented imaginary ones because I hoped that to go over a passage or a whole chorus again and again might result in a more lasting impact on youthful minds and spirits. This music asks more than rehearsing; it must be literally absorbed through days and weeks and even years of experience. I do not in the slightest degree believe that great music can, all by itself, exert a beneficent moral influence; but I do know that to sing one of the major choral works of Bach, to live for a space in a musical eloquence that has no superior, to be permitted to share the thoughts of one whose genius knew no limits, to sense that one has played an active role in re-creating a timeless work of art—an experience like this, I say, offers us a lasting resource of life and leaves us at least different beings from what we were before.

2

Whatever capacities you discover in Bach and Handel which set them above or apart from their predecessors and contemporaries may be accounted for partly by their experience of music past and present, partly by the operation of their own particular genius, and partly by their superlative handling of contemporary resource—a skill resulting, presumably, from a normal, progressive education in music beginning early in life and carried on for some time, at least, under systematic teaching. The record of Handel's early studies is relatively easy to follow, and the various musical influences that were brought to bear on him in the course of his career are fairly plain reading. Indeed, Handel's music does not offer much ground for speculation; his technique was basically that of the thorough-bass period, and his musical ideas and language are in accord with the ideals of that period—a fact which throws some light on his popularity in his own day. One would hesitate to say that his imagination was more restricted or his musical ideas less important than those of Bach, yet the fact remains that we can account for all the music of Handel; we can explain it because, allow-ing for that indeterminate factor of genius, we know the steps by which he advanced to become the composer which, in the end, he was.

But with Bach it is far different. We have no proper record of his early studies and only the vaguest information as to how he built up his technical armory. Viewed simply as tech-nical achievement, as absolute mastery over the materials of music, the compositions of Bach are an unending source of wonder; the more so when we compare the apparently slight formal training from which Bach benefited with the long and elaborate discipline expected of those in our own time whom we call composers. We are told that Johann Sebastian was preceded by a formidably long line of musical ancestors who bequeathed to him, through successive generations of Bachs, what we commonly call a "gift for music"; that at the age of ten, being left an orphan and taken into the household of an elder brother who was an organist of some distinction, the young Bach profited from hearing a great deal of solid Ger-man musical art, particularly of the church variety; that he sang for a number of years in choirs, thereby gaining an in-sight into the subtleties of choral composition and a sympa-thetic approach, as a composer, to the problems of choral style—and that, I may say, puts a heavy burden on the cred-ulousness of the conductor and singer of Bach's music. We know with what zeal he copied the works of other musicians, and this device is known to be a valuable ally to technical training. But the practical inquirer who has himself struggled to gain some command over the intricacies involved in the writing of simple three-part counterpoint will hardly be con-tent with the explanation that that colossal monument of contrapuntal legerdemain known as the *Art of Fugue* resulted from any such absorptive process of education as is represented by listening to music, by copying it, or by the happy accident of a musical heritage. The mystery is the more profound because Bach seems to have entered on a professional career at about the time of life when the modern student is concerned with developing his musical powers. The biographers have undoubtedly told the story as fully as human industry makes possible, and we can only wish in vain that Bach had kept a journal of his activities, beginning with his early years and continuing to the end. It seems incredible that Bach should have journeyed to Lübeck to hear Buxtehude play, and presumably to meet him, and that after a sojourn in Lübeck he should have returned to his post without having detailed instruction from Buxtehude; but there is no evidence that Buxtehude was ever Bach's teacher. Only Bach himself could have enlightened us as to the educational processes through which he passed. Only in that way could we know who corrected his first set of parallels, and through what succeeding stages he arrived at technical completeness.

We have it on the authority of Terry that Bach was once interrogated as to the secret of his power. Here, indeed, was an earth-shaking opportunity, and it is not difficult to imagine the spirits of all who were to follow him, historians, teachers, students, composers, theorists, standing in eager expectation, notebook in hand, awaiting the revelation that would unlock the mystery of technical perfection and chart the ideal course of music education. Bach's reply was simply this: "I worked hard." [12] May I say that as a summons to succeeding generations to plunge blindly up the slopes of Parnassus without benefit of guide, staff, or trail, that answer stands as the ultimate in pedagogic frustration. No composer whose musical speech even approaches that of Bach in profundity has been as reticent as he in explaining his position with regard to his own music. There is a multitude of significances in that music for which his biographers supply no reasonable background. I have mentioned his habit of copying the music of others; and all organists are familiar with the fact that he drew on Legrenzi for the subject of the C minor Double Fugue, and on Raison for the idea of the theme of the C minor Passacaglia, and on Reinken for the outline of the subject of the great G minor Fugue; and these constitute irrefutable evidence of a very obvious kind of influence on Bach. We are told that he was acquainted with the music of a small host of composers, that he copied not a little of it, and that he undoubtedly studied that part of it which he thought important for himself. Among these composers were Palestrina, Lotti, Corelli, Vivaldi, Couperin, Fux, Caldara, Handel, the two Grauns, Frescobaldi, Keiser, Hasse, Telemann, Pachelbel, Grigny, Dieuport, D'Anglebert, Froberger, Buxtehude, Marcello, and Kerll, all here presented in scrambled succession the more to emphasize their diversity of time and place. Nor does this represent the feverish activity of a young student eager to acquaint himself with the music of others. "Throughout his life," says the *Bach Reader*, "he showed an insatiable interest in all kinds of music, old and new, and of all nations." [13] That the traces of exterior influence are manifestly present in Bach's style is admitted, but it is the unrecorded and perhaps undiscoverable influences that I find profoundly interesting. For example, Schweitzer states that Pitschel, a contemporary of Bach in Leipzig, declared that when Bach was about to improvise, it was his custom ordinarily to play from the score a composition by another composer; [14] the implication being that Bach needed to spark his own invention with some outside stimulus. This does, indeed, suggest a strong similarity between the types of imagination possessed by Bach and by Coleridge. Most of Bach's library being long ago widely dispersed, it is probably too late for anyone to do for Bach what John Livingston Lowes did for Coleridge in *The Road to Xanadu*—ferret out every discoverable influence to which Bach was subjected which might be reflected in his music. We shall never know how Bach won his technical supremacy, nor all that went into the making of his total art. What we do know may well lead us to suspect that there are still undiscovered forces that helped to mold his style.

Bach came at the end of a period in which form was a detail to a very great extent categorically treated. Once forms and types were established, there seems to have been little inclination to depart from them. Yet one of the invariably impressive features of Bach's music is his handling of form, because the function of form in his music is not the setting of a predestined mold into which the music should be poured; it was to be a strong but flexible frame for the musical ideas and their working out. Bach must have been thoroughly imbued with the baroque idea of form; nonetheless, he was forever departing from it. Take his St. Anne Fugue for the organ. This is a long work in three well-defined sections, and in selecting such a plan for the St. Anne, Bach was tempting fate, for it was the periodic character of the writing in imitative types from the ricercar on, as well as the use of a sectionalized scheme for the fugue, that had resulted in a lack of continuity in the writing of Bach's predecessors; and it was continuity, in a very real sense, that Bach had himself introduced into the fugue. Why he chose three sections is not known, but it has been surmised that this arrangement was characteristic of Bach in its suggestion of the three persons of the Trinity. With three separate subjects at his disposal, Bach

31

would normally have written a triple fugue in which, at some point, all three subjects would be sounded together, but he does not do this, and it is useless to ask why Bach treated the material of the St. Anne Fugue as he did. One can only say that it suited him to do so, and that his choice was justified, for in the St. Anne he left us one of the most stupendous and artistically satisfying of his fugal creations.

Or consider the Little G minor, so called, also for the organ. Here is a fugue much shorter than the St. Anne and corresponding in style to the conventional baroque type. It has been called defective because it fails to conform to all the specifications of a fugue: the subject is once presented incomplete, and the stretto, which does not come at the place usually appointed for it, is not much more than an intimation of a stretto. If these are defects, they are so only to the analyst, for the Little G minor is frequently played and is an unfailing source of delight to both performer and listener. Both the St. Anne and the Little G minor *are* fugues, and both are eloquent of the freedom and individuality with which Bach treated the whole problem of form.

Forms are considered to be really confining when they offer the composer, for expansion, given material which he must treat without change in its successive appearances. One of the most inflexible and forbidding of these is the passacaglia, which is, basically, a melodic formula, repeated, generally in the bass, as many times as the composer may choose. Over this formula varied and increasingly interesting musical substance must be written. No composer, unless his imaginative and technical resources are absolutely unlimited, will embark on the composition of a passacaglia, and even so he will hardly select that form as the conveyance for feelings which demand the utmost freedom in expression. Yet Bach, when he came to set the "Crucifixus" in the *B minor Mass*, certainly one of the most poignant of all texts, deliberately chose to restrict himself to the ironclad conventions of the passacaglia form. Again, it is the eye alone that reveals the form, for to the ear text, form, and music seem to be so providentially predestined for one another that every composer of Masses from Bach's time to this must have wondered if he ought not to set his Crucifixus as a passacaglia.

Bach's expansion of types long established, types such as the variation and the dance, displays still another aspect of his attitude towards form. The variation, allied in nature to the passacaglia, has been a perpetual challenge to the ingenuity of composers. The melody which constituted the given factor in a work was at first varied in somewhat obvious ways, but throughout the baroque period its treatment grew in subtlety. Bach, though he seems not to have had a great interest in the variation form, did by no means neglect it, and he left us one set, the monumental *Goldberg Variations*, written on a theme from the *Klavierbüchlein* of Anna Magdalena Bach, which in their ingenuity and resource far overtop all their predecessors and are rivaled only, perhaps, by the *Diabelli Variations* of Beethoven. Dance movements, which began as brief, purely functional pieces, had risen to the status of artistic productions in the hands of great sixteenth-century composers like William Byrd, and in the partitas of Bach the ideal finds its fulfillment. An allemande, for example, retains the meter traditionally assigned to it, and that is almost its only contact with its ancestor. In all particulars it assumes a musical importance and displays such breadth of treatment that the hearer, seeking a title for it, would never suspect that its humble origin would be found in the dance.

Another detail which can be explained only in the light

33

of the individual talent of Bach and Handel is their use of rhythm, and as a point of departure for a treatment of this I should like to take the concerto grosso, as it is found in these two composers. In the concerto grosso a small body of instruments was treated as a solo group, and against these was set the remainder of the orchestra as an accompaniment. The solo group was called the concertino and the larger accompanying group was called the ripieno or tutti. Corelli and Vivaldi in their concerti grossi prepared the way for a more varied and extended treatment of the form by Bach and Handel. Corelli's twelve concerti grossi carry over the trio sonata idea into the concerto form, his solo group consisting of two violins and a violoncello; this or a comparable grouping being generally typical of the concertino in pre-Bach and Handel practice. Although Corelli and Vivaldi were contemporaries, the former being born in 1653 and the latter about 1675, their musical viewpoints, like those of Bach and Handel, were different. Corelli was the conservative, and in some respects his music sounds earlier than its time. It is in the true thorough-bass tradition, but it does possess a closer affinity with vocal style than does the music of Vivaldi. The latter was more progressive in his use of harmony as well as in other respects, though the chief virtues of his music are not, perhaps, to be found in its substance but rather in its highly effective brilliance. Handel inclined to the idea of the string concertino, but Bach saw in the medium of a group of solo instruments an opportunity to increase effectiveness by the inclusion in the concertino of instruments other than strings—instruments such as the oboe, flute, trumpet, and horn—thus adding immeasurably to musical interest by setting one instrumental color against another instead of relying on the contrast obtained by opposing a smaller against a larger group of instruments of identical timbre and technique.

34

The six Brandenburg Concertos, written when Bach w̶
thirty-six years old, were composed at the request of the
Margrave Christian Ludwig of Brandenburg and were des-
patched to that worthy in 1721. As far as is known, Bach
never received any notification of their receipt, nor is there
any record of his being rewarded in any way for his work. It
is even possible that these concertos were never performed
during Bach's lifetime, for when, at the Margrave's death,
these works were catalogued as a part of his library, they
were lumped together with the music of assorted composers
and valued at almost nothing. What sort of man this Christian
Ludwig was I cannot say, but I have often thought that it
would have been the neatest stroke of poetic justice if he
could have known that for posterity his sole distinction would
lie in his having possessed the first autograph copy of the
immortal Brandenburg Concertos. Whether or not the Margrave thought well of them, Bach certainly did, for on more
than one occasion he borrowed material from them to use in
his cantatas.

Handel composed three sets of concerti grossi. The first
set are known as the "oboe" concertos, and in these the concertino included oboes, flutes, and bassoons. Another set, published with the works of other composers under the title
"Select Harmony," again included oboes. In his third and
greatest collection, however, known as the "Twelve Grand
Concertos" and published in 1740, he confined himself entirely to strings both in the concertino and in the ripieno.
His abandonment, in these concertos, of the resource of color
offered by the employment of wind instruments is significant
because it shows how confident Handel must have been of
the charm of his music when he could confine himself to the
medium of a single timbre.

Possibly because of the complex contrapuntal organization which is common to Bach's concerti grossi, a comparison of these works with his compositions for organ has been suggested. In the concertos, however, the scope of orchestral technique transcends the limits of what may be achieved on the organ by ten fingers and two feet. Of the resources offered by the orchestra, the diversity of technique, the peculiar properties of color belonging to the different instruments, and above all the opportunity for exploiting a marked and even a percussive rhythm impossible to produce on the organ —of all these Bach took the greatest advantage.

The string writing of Corelli compared with that of Bach and Handel seems restricted. He does not avail himself of the wider range and technical potentialities of the instruments as they do, and this is the more striking in Handel's case because of his adherence to the exclusively string scoring of his predecessor. Indeed, one feels that the space of time which separates Corelli from Handel might well be much greater than it is in view of the added boldness and vigor of Handel's writing, the difference between their melodic procedures, Handel's broader harmonic outlook, and his more highly developed sense of organization. The concerti grossi of Handel and Bach not only offer an interesting contrast to the work of their predecessors but also furnish a valid basis for comparing certain details of the work of the two composers themselves. Some of these differences have been mentioned in connection with their choral music, but one other, namely their respective employment of the element of rhythm, I should now like to take up. I did not mention this in connection with the choral music because choral music is not a just determinant of rhythmic practice, inasmuch as no composer is rhythmically free when setting a text to music. Words and the requirements they make with regard to accent exert a definite control over rhythmic procedure. In purely instrumental music, on the other hand, the composer, being limited only by his capacity in that direction, may indulge his feeling for rhythm to any extent he may choose. The music of both Bach and Handel is strongly rhythmic but in different ways. With Handel the rhythm seems to be like his counterpoint or his phraseology—that is, merely another ingredient in the composition. But with Bach it is impossible to disassociate the rhythm from the remaining substance of his music. The rhythm is, to be sure, a presence vividly felt, but it is so doweled into all the other features that it seems to grow out of them and to be a part of the total structure of the music. It would be impossible to overemphasize Bach's fondness for strong rhythm. Only Handel, certainly, among his contemporaries had it in anything like the same degree. Sometimes, in Bach's music, the element of rhythm is so important that it appears to be the dominant consideration. Take, for example, the harpsichord concerto in D. That work comes very near to being rhythm in the abstract. Allowing for the due presence of other components such as harmony or melody, it is the rhythm which exceeds all other interests. Bach's enthusiasm for Italian music is reflected in his own work, but his grasp of the vitalizing power of rhythm and his ability to invoke it took him far beyond the Italian concept. He must have admired greatly the concertos of Vivaldi, for he adopted some twenty of these, at the same time changing them to conform to his own ideas. The concerto in A minor is a good example of the superimposition by Bach of his love of a driving, pulsatile rhythm on the even rhythmic flow that generally pervades the music of the thorough-bass era. Vivaldi wrote his concerto for four violins; Bach arranged it as a concerto for four harpsichords, and the implications of the change are at once obvious. You have only to take a single page from the Vivaldi original and compare it with the identical page in Bach's arrangement to observe to what an extent the pulse is intensified by the substitution of the sharp strokes of the harpsichord for the milder accent of the strings.

In pages like that Bach approaches nearest to Handel's rhythmic method. Partly because Handel was so often, for dramatic as well as musical reasons, predominantly harmonic in his procedure, the rhythmic pulse is generally heard. Bach's harpsichord concerto in D and his four-harpsichord concerto in A do, as I have stated, illustrate his predilection for strong rhythms, but it is when he disperses the rhythm through the infinite complexities of his counterpoint without once departing from the sense of a driving and relentless pulse that the true power of Bach the rhythmist is revealed. On the whole, one would say that Handel's rhythm is broad, sweeping, and vigorous, while Bach's is incisive and almost hypnotic in its insistence. In the chorus "Worthy Is the Lamb" from *Messiah*, Handel is his typical, majestic, rhythmic self—the pulses sometimes widely separated and occasionally of unequal length; a rhythmic treatment comparatively rare with Bach save occasionally in the organ music. Outside the instrumental field I know of no examples so useful for comparison in this matter as the choruses "Then Round About the Starry Throne" of Handel and the "Et expecto" from Bach's *B minor Mass*. Without attempting to make a technical distinction it is enough to say that one is deeply impressed but not transported by Handel's rhythm, whereas in the Bach chorus the irresistibly compelling impact of the beat, driving the music forward without rest, so conduces to bodily motion, so engrosses the listener, that the man who is not clay must keep a tight rein on himself if he is not to become a serious distraction to his neighbors in the concert hall.

Handel is not at his best either rhythmically or substantially in his works for harpsichord. He was, perhaps, inhibited by the fragility of that instrument; indeed, one can almost visualize it shrinking before his threatening figure. To whatever cause it may be ascribed, the fact remains that in the harpsichord music, in spite of delightful movements from the suites, Handel seems less than himself. Skillfully composed, the music is urbane and delightful, but it represents Handel as a continuer rather than as a consummator of baroque keyboard tradition. The organ concertos are another matter. The style of organ writing, to be sure, is far different from that of Bach in that it lies close to the harpsichord; and this is to be expected because Handel designed his organ concertos for performance either on the harpsichord or on the organ. In those concertos, however, Handel had at his command, when he wished for them, a powerful instrument and the resources of the orchestra as accompaniment. Whether Handel willingly cast these concertos for use on either instrument we do not know, but he could hardly have issued them as playable on the complete organ, for it was rare to find a pedal board on the English instrument of his day. He performed them frequently between the parts of his oratorios, and the form in which we have them probably represents only a fraction of what they really were when filled out with the improvisations which Handel was so fond of adding. For Bach, the organ was associated with the church, and Handel's employment of it as a means of entertainment would doubtless not have appealed to Bach. Furthermore, it is probable that Bach held the organ in such high regard as a solo instrument that he preferred its voice to sound alone, undistracted by competition with other instruments.

All in all, Handel's fame rests largely on his concerti grossi, his operas, and particularly his oratorios. It is in the arias of the operas that Handel displays the essence of his vocal power, a power which in the beginning he did not possess but which he acquired in great degree from a study of Italian style. His treatment of the aria, however, goes far beyond the Italian achievement, because he added to Italian melodiousness the idiomatic quality of his own melodic genius, in something the same way that Mozart glorified the Italian melody of his time. Choruses were not a feature of the opera as they were of the oratorio, being generally replaced by ensembles of soloists—partly, no doubt, for reasons of economy but also, as we may suppose, because each singer preferred to be heard as nearly as possible all by himself. Probably not since the Middle Ages had singers been in such a position of command. Operas were literally constructed about them. Each work called for three women singers and three or four men singers. There were five different types of arias and they were distributed in a practically fixed order throughout an opera. The da capo, prime enemy of dramatic logic, was a relatively constant feature. To a man of Handel's independent character all this must have been irksome, and he did not feel himself bound to observe tradition in all respects. Occasional revivals are revelations of the amazing amount of superb music contained in these operas. Among the finest are *Rinaldo*, *Julius Caesar*, and *Xerxes*, the last of which contains the famous aria "My Plane Tree" to which, under the title of Handel's "Largo," some of us have been married and all of us will be buried. The miracle is that in spite of the rapidity with which Handel composed, there is no lapse in the fineness of the workmanship. *Rinaldo*, for example, was composed in fourteen days and is exceeded in artistic prestidigitation only by the monumental *Messiah*, which required just twenty-four days for its completion. Handel, to be sure, was a perennial borrower of music not only from himself but from other composers as well; even so, we must marvel at the skill which made it possible to organize and score such extensive compositions in so short a period of time.

In referring to Handel as a borrower I am not unaware that his wholesale and brazen use of the music of others, sometimes without change and never, so far as I know, with acknowledgment, has led to his being characterized so harshly that the word "borrower" may be taken as the most pallid of euphemisms. The indisputable fact that he generally converted what he took into something far superior to the original has been put forward in justification of his behavior; justification on aesthetic grounds, perhaps, but certainly not in the sphere of ethics. One scholar has compiled a list of twenty-nine composers upon whose music Handel drew, and after the last composer named he has cautiously added "et cetera." To the "et cetera" I once added a name on my own account. There is a passage in Handel's *Burial Anthem* which, when I first came across it, seemed to be anachronistic because it was purely modal in style, and modality had ceased to be an element in composition by Handel's time. Being acquainted with a motet by Jacob Handl, a composer of the sixteenth century, in which there were certain textual coincidences with the later piece, I compared the two; and there, in at least one instance in the composition of G. F. Handel, note for note and word for word, was the music of Jacob Handl. I doubt not that others had detected the identity long before I did, but the excited and perhaps regretful surprise of the first discoverer could hardly have been greater than mine.

There was disapproval of musical plagiarism in the eighteenth century, and though Handel seems largely to have escaped reproach, that was probably because his pilferings came to light mainly after his death. It is not by way of extenuation to say that the constant pressure on him to produce new music may have led him to supply his needs partly from the musical stock of other composers. Nonetheless, in my veneration for those attributes of character which, in spite of this defect, still display him as a heroic figure, I like to think that it was mainly practical need that influenced his conduct. Surely, the genius and innate originality of which he was possessed would definitely suggest that unless forced by exterior circumstance, he had no need of looking outside himself for the materials of his music.[15]

When Handel first came to England in 1710—he subsequently became a naturalized English citizen in 1726—the doors of opportunity opened for English music. Since the days of Purcell there had been no native English opera worthy of the name, and Handel, who had studied Purcell's music and who was a good judge of English musical taste, could as an adopted son have inaugurated the Golden Age of English opera. But Handel was saturated with Italian style and too firmly committed to the Italian type of opera to adapt himself to new musical circumstances, and the opportunity, regrettably, was lost. Actually, Handel's influence on English music, like Mendelssohn's at a later time, was both extensive and devastating. Both composers were choral magicians, and their skill invoked a host of English imitators, none of whom even remotely rivaled either Handel or Mendelssohn as composers. Mendelssohn's influence was, to be sure, more debilitating than Handel's because, while the exteriors of the latter's style were not difficult to assimilate, a fair imitation of them occasionally imparting a slight degree of verisimilitude to the copy, Mendelssohn's correct, orthodox musical language, expressed in a choral technique that has known few equals, simply subjugated the English ear and unleashed a flood of watered-down likenesses of Mendelssohn's style that to this day trickle through the choir lofts of musically unenlightened churches.

It seems strange that the products of the greatest German oratorio composer of his time should have been little heard in the country of his birth. *Messiah*, for example, went largely unrecognized in Germany until after Mozart had revived it in Vienna in 1789. It was the English who really appreciated Handel's oratorios, and in writing them he justified his adopted citizenship and more than compensated for his neglect of native English opera. It is out of the oratorios that the real Handel finally shines forth. He was fifty-three when he turned from the writing of operas to cultivate the oratorio, and in his exploitation of this form may be seen the results of his cosmopolitan training as well as the expression of his personality. They bear eloquent witness to Handel's musical nature which had its roots in the technical thoroughness and German solidity of style that came from his early training under Zachau, who in spite of his admirable and sorely neglected music will probably endure in memory mainly as Handel's teacher. To Handel's German equipment may be added a mastery of Italian style acquired during the time he spent in that country, and a complete understanding of English choral art, especially as it is manifested in Purcell. Most important of all, however, is Handel himself, who invested everything he wrote with a spaciousness and a majesty that came only from his own genius. Within the years 1738 to 1757, a period devoted almost exclusively to oratorio composition, are concentrated his major achievements as a composer: *Saul, Israel in Egypt, Samson, Messiah, Joshua, Solomon, Jeptha,* and the *Triumph of Time and Truth,* each one a masterpiece. The chorus, which from relatively early in the baroque period had been a much emphasized feature of the oratorio, and one of the characterizing differences between that form and the opera, reaches its apotheosis in Handel's oratorios. In *Israel in Egypt,* for example, the choruses furnish by far the larger part of the interest.

Handel's choruses, however, are more than music; they reveal in their massiveness and their power the man himself, energetic, pompous, magnificent, and above all undefeatable. A great many years ago I was fortunate enough to have put at my disposal in the British Museum the collection of autograph manuscripts of the oratorios. Eventually I came to a study of *Jeptha* and had proceeded some distance through it when I began to observe strange irregularities in the notation: stems placed at some distance from the notes to which they belonged, and notes which had obviously lost their way and had become misplaced. The writing became more and more incomplete and obscure until finally it straggled away into nothing. At the bottom of the page was a scribbled note in German which read, in effect: "I cannot go on—my left eye is too bad." Handel was going blind. As I held the page in my hand I wondered if he had done as you or I would have done, abandoned the project forever in an effort to salvage his remaining eyesight; but knowing Handel's rugged and determined character I could hardly imagine his declaring a truce with fate. Would he not persist, like Milton hastening to finish the *First Defense of the English People* before darkness should overtake him? The oratorio had, of course, been completed, but the remainder might well have been dictated

44

to an amanuensis. It was not. When I turned the page over, there was more music in Handel's handwriting, dated ten days later than the preceding page, and another little note the sense of which was: "Feeling better. At work again." [16] And because all that indomitableness is in Handel's music, his art would have to be deficient in many respects to cause it to fall short of utter greatness.

Quite the best characterization of Handel I have read appeared in a book entitled *Old Scores and New Readings* by the English critic John Runciman, and I cannot do better than to quote from his essay.

"Mr. George Frideric Handel is by far the most superb personage one meets in the history of music. He alone of all the musicians lived his life straight through in the grand manner. Spohr had dignity; Gluck insisted upon respect being shown a man of his talent; Spontini was sufficiently self-assertive; Beethoven treated his noble patrons as so many handfuls of dirt. But it is impossible altogether to lose sight of the peasant in Beethoven and Gluck; Spohr had more than a trace of the successful shopkeeper; Spontini's assertion often became mere insufferable bumptiousness. Besides, they all won their positions through being the best men in the field, and they held them with a proud consciousness of being the best men. But in Handel we have a polished gentleman, a lord amongst lords, almost a king amongst kings; and had his musical powers been much smaller than they were, he might quite possibly have gained and held his position just the same. He slighted the Elector of Hanover; and when that noble creature became George I. of England, Handel had only to do the handsome thing, as a handsome gentleman should, to be immediately taken back into favour. He was educated— was, in fact, a university man of the German sort; he could

45

write and spell, and add up rows of figures, and had many other accomplishments which gentlemen of the period affected a little to despise. He had a pungent and a copious wit. He had quite a commercial genius; he was an impresario, and had engagements to offer other people instead of having to beg for engagements for himself; and he was always treated by the British with all the respect they keep for the man who has made money, or, having lost it, is fast making it again. He fought for the lordship of opera against nearly the whole English nobility, and they paid him the compliment of banding together with as much ado to ruin him as if their purpose had been to drive his royal master from the throne. He treated all opposition with a splendid good-humoured disdain. If his theatre was empty, then the music sounded the better. If a singer threatened to jump on the harpsichord because Handel's accompaniments attracted more notice than the singing, Handel asked for the date of the proposed performance that it might be advertised, for more people would come to see the singer jump than hear him sing. He was, in short, a most superb person, quite the grand seigneur. Think of Bach, the little shabby unimportant cantor, or of Beethoven, important enough but shabby, and with a great sorrow in his eyes, and an air of weariness, almost of defeat. Then look at the magnificent Mr. Handel in Hudson's portrait: fashionably dressed in a great periwig and gorgeous scarlet coat, victorious, energetic, self-possessed, self-confident, self-satisfied, jovial, and proud as Beelzebub (to use his own comparison)—too proud to ask for recognition were homage refused. . . .

"But his lofty position was not entirely due to his overwhelming personality. His intellect, if less vast, less comprehensive, than Beethoven's, was less like the intellect of a great peasant: it was swifter, keener, surer. Where Beethoven plodded, Handel leaped. And a degree of genius which did nothing for Bach, a little for Mozart, and all for Beethoven, did something for Handel. Without a voice worth taking into consideration, he could, and at least on one occasion did, sing so touchingly that the leading singer of the age dared not risk his reputation by singing after him. He was not only the first composer of the day, but also the first organist and the first harpsichord player; for his only possible rival, Sebastian Bach, was an obscure schoolmaster in a small, nearly un-heard-of, German town. And so personal force, musical genius, business talent, education, and general brain power went to the making of a man who hobnobbed with dukes and kings, who ruled musical England with an iron rule, who threatened to throw distinguished soprano ladies from windows, and was threatened with never an action for battery in return, who went through the world with a regal gait, and was, in a word, the most astonishing lord of music the world has seen." [17]

3

It would be artificial to deal with Bach's advances in formal matters as though they represented an issue to be considered by itself. We take the form for granted because, with Bach, form and substance are one. The music is what we hear, and it is the sum of the manifold details, technical and psychological, which make up that music which is of first importance. One of the most convincing evidences of this composer's regard for unity in a composition, his insistence that every note shall bear some relation to the musical meaning, is seen in the character of the melodic tracery which he knew so well how to weave. And here again he advances far beyond his predecessors and contemporaries. Decorative passages could be either a means to the display of virtuosity or to the gaining of variety through contrast with cantabile writing. In Bach's case they may be either, but they are always something more. It sounds anomalous to speak of a single note as having a destiny, and yet that is what seems to happen so often in Bach's lyric slow movements. Held notes are separated from one another and must be bridged in some way. The period possessed an abundant resource of ornamental patterns and devices which could be utilized, but so often they seem like an end in themselves and not especially germane to the chief musical idea. One feels that with Bach, however, the single note is like a plant waiting impatiently to burst forth, not with *any* flowers, but with those blooms which that particular growth only could produce; and once it has revealed its full flowering it merges into another note which then may blossom in its turn. Thus the decoration, which even to the eye is impressive in its contour, when heard not only ministers to grace and beauty but at the same time adds to the music both congruity and unity.

Another striking facet of Bach's genius is his capacity for building an imposing musical structure out of elementary and sometimes even unpromising material. Occasionally, as in the great D major organ fugue, he lights on a simple motif, and as though trying to show how exciting and convincing mere repetition may be, he works it over and over until it would appear that with one more appearance he would grind it to powder. Or he will adopt a single device such as the auxiliary note, the last resort of the harried composer who must set up some sort of rhythmic stir in his music; or an arpeggio, or a scale; all of them, at first glance, quite unprovocative musical material, and from these he will construct music of significance and beauty. The Third Brandenburg Concerto is literally a treatise on how to glorify the technically commonplace. But in the D major fugue in the second book of the *Well-Tempered Clavichord* Bach carries this principle to its highest manifestation. This fugue is constructed on two motifs, neither of which suggests any bright future for itself as material for development. Furthermore, Bach is unremitting in his insistence on them. G. W. Woodworth has pointed out that motif no. 1 occurs twenty-four times, and motif no. 2 one hundred and five times, and all within the space of four minutes. Yet out of so little Bach has evolved a work of absorbing interest, strong emotional appeal, and technical perfection. Here again, in terms of beauty, is wrought the miracle of the loaves and fishes.

There is another characteristic of Bach's music that is, I think, most nearly paralleled in Mozart's work, namely what, for want of a better term, I will designate as "nonstop," by which I mean that with the first note a spring is released which projects the music forward continuously until we bring up against the double bar with an impact that is almost physical. There is no hesitation, no calculation; the last note is prophesied by the first. The energy and drive which Bach displays in music of this kind is overwhelming and conduces to exhaustion on the part of both performers and listeners. But whether the music is characterized by energy, continuity of thought, feeling for proportion, or any other factor, or the sum of all of them, sooner or later we find ourselves speculating as to the steps by which Bach learned to employ these qualities so impressively and the degrees by which he advanced to the complete technical mastery that was his. As I have said before, we shall never know all that went into the fullness of Bach's art, because accurate and detailed knowledge of its sources never has existed. I want now to revert to that mystery, speaking of perhaps the most unexplainable of his gifts, his sense of the dramatic. I am thinking especially of the Passions, and of the *St. Matthew* in particular.

The two great forms, the Mass and the Passion, unquestionably invite dramatic treatment. In more than one ecclesiastical observance, indeed, there lies the suggestion of a

51

symbolism that is dramatic in itself. Take, for example, the ceremonial of the candles at the Maunday Thursday service, when the flames are gradually extinguished until but one remains, this last one to be finally removed from sight to symbolize for us the passing of the Light of the World. Although Luther transferred the Mass with modifications to the use of the Reformed service, in replacing the Offertorium of the Mass by the sermon he performed a characteristically Protestant act, for he deleted a moment of dramatic significance. May I venture the admittedly impertinent opinion that in so doing, Luther, from the point of view of continuity and climax, fundamental concepts in any religious observance, did us a marked disservice. Theological necessity perhaps left him no alternative, but beginning with that alteration the typical Protestant service has gradually come to disregard any logical succession in its parts, with a corresponding neglect of anything like climax, which is a strong feature in the Mass. The crucial act in the Protestant service is the sermon; and I can only say of the sermon, having listened during one measurable period of my life to twelve of them each week, that it is often the very annihilation of climax.

In spite of gestures and the scenic character of its vestments, the Mass never really becomes a drama because, as Karl Young says in his book *The Drama of the Medieval Church*, "Dramatic externalities must not be taken for genuine drama itself, in which the essential element is not forms of speech and movement, but *impersonation*." [18] And later he restates his conviction that the Mass must be excluded from consideration as drama because it is not, as he says, "a representation of an action, but an actual recreation of it." [19] The Passion, however, is a drama. Here is no celebrant acting in place of Christ; there is a singer who impersonates him, and the taking of that step must have involved considerable daring. Karl Young believes that the representation of the last events in Christ's life was not welcome as a part of ecclesiastical observance, and he comments on the late adoption of the Passion story, as a play, by the Church. In this we are reminded of the tardy employment of counterpoint as a musical vehicle for the Mass; perhaps it was felt that the sanctity of that text, once it had been separated from its simpler conveyance, was in danger of losing something of its integrity. In any case, no pressing need was felt, apparently, for submitting the Passion account to actual stage production, for, as Young points out, the death of Christ could be daily presented in the Mass itself.[20]

The *St. Matthew* is a dramatic work, and the first difficulty which Bach faced in the organization of it was to infuse continuity and climax into a collection of hopelessly disparate elements: narrative, commentary, grief, tragedy, resignation, violence, and meditation. With the exception of the last, one might say that Bach was in a no more taxing situation than the opera composers of his day. It was the chorale, however, constantly interjected throughout the story, which superficially viewed was the enemy of dramatic unity. The chorales represent, to a great extent, the meditative element, and as such would appear to be an unwarranted interruption of dramatic progress; but upon examination they prove to be, both in text and music, most apposite links between the sections of the work. Bach used the music of the Passion chorale five times in the *St. Matthew;* similarly, the melody "Herzliebster Jesu" is introduced three times and "Welt, sieh' hier dein Leben" twice. Thus these chorales have actual dramatic virtue, as the repeated ritornelli do in Monteverdi's *Orfeo,* reminding us of the tragic continuity of the story. Incidentally, among his predecessors, Bach would appear to have the closest affinity with Monteverdi and Schütz in the expression of sheer unadorned dramatic truth. The latter's setting of "Saul, Saul, Why Persecutest Thou Me," while great in its own right, is nonetheless the voice of John preparing the way. Yet Bach probably never heard of Monteverdi, and if he knew the music of Schütz he would seem not to have had a high regard for it.

Outside the Passions I know of only one instance of the use of the interruptive technique under dramatic circumstances, and that is in an oratorio or, better, cantata, entitled *A Child of Our Time* published in 1944, both text and music by the English composer Michael Tippett.[21] Negro spirituals are interspersed throughout the work, the texts of these pointing up the ideas which precede them. This is a very interesting attempt to transfer Bach's method to the area of secular music, but there is at least one obstacle to its accomplishment. The spiritual is an idiomatic musical type; it is only really itself when it stands quite alone, and it is, as more than one composer has discovered, congenitally unincorporable into alien musical material. The chorales and the remainder of the music in the *St. Matthew* are homogeneous in style, while the overornate treatment of the spirituals in *A Child of Our Time*, set in the midst of contemporary musical language, only serves to emphasize the artificiality of the role they are called upon to play. The hands are the hands of Bach, but the voice, alas, is far from being his.

How much the key scheme which Bach employed for the *St. Matthew* ministers not only to its organizational integrity but also to its dramatic coherence is not realized until one makes a close study of this feature. The composer must have planned his key succession with elaborate care, for it is often

54

evident, especially at the end of recitatives or even of larger movements, that he was preparing the tonality that seemed best suited to the mood of the text. The case of the Passion chorale is interesting. The first three appearances of it are in E, E flat, and D respectively. Then, after the account of the smiting of Jesus, comes F, the highest of all, in a harmonization that is tense and which takes the voices into a relatively high range. The vocal color alone gives evidence of mounting drama. And finally, just after the death of Jesus, Bach uses A, the lowest key of the five, and puts the voices in a subdued range. At the end he treats the melody in the Phrygian mode which, by its remoteness from the everyday experience of major and minor, creates an atmosphere of unearthly detachment.

It is profitable to put oneself in Bach's place when he was faced with the problem of how to go on after the climactic point in the story had been reached. Let me point out how some other composers have met the issue. The more modern versions of the Passion story, of which Gounod's *Redemption* and Dubois's *Seven Last Words* are typical, immediately take full advantage of the pictorial and melodramatic possibilities of the scene; but one of the most impressive of the later settings, a Passion by Kurt Thomas, published in 1926, returns, interestingly enough, to the motet form of the sixteenth century and thereby denies itself the dramatic resources which would be contributed by an instrumental accompaniment. The rending of the veil is dealt with in a brief passage in contrapuntal imitation which hardly transcends the sphere of animated narrative. Of the Passions just preceding those of Bach, the two most important are those of Sebastiani and Theile. Theile, who in 1673 published a *Passion According to St. Matthew*, does proceed immediately with a continuation, in recitative, of the account of the crucifixion. Sebastiani, however, who had brought out in 1672 another Passion on the St. Matthew text, prophesies Bach's method most appropriately by introducing after the crucifixion the chorale "In Peace and Joy I Now Depart"; and this is followed by a thoroughly matter-of-fact recitative dealing with the rending of the veil. Bach, then, was not the first to perceive the effectiveness of introducing a chorale after the crucifixion, but his masterly handling of that technique makes of the Passion chorale more than a contrast or a relief; it takes on a tremendous dramatic significance—a significance which one might reasonably assume to have disappeared after four previous hearings of the melody. Brockes' poem, which Handel adopted for *his* setting of the Passion, makes no reference to the rending. Instead it introduces a text beginning "Rise, Powers Infernal," words which fitted Handel as neatly as his wig, and to which he wrote a tenor solo that might have come from any of his operas. Donald Tovey once wrote, "To disagree with Schweitzer is dangerously like disagreeing with Bach." [22] Even more rebellious is it, I suppose, to disagree with Bach about Bach, but I timidly confess that for me the one disappointing page in the *St. Matthew* is that which describes the rending of the veil. That scene precedes Christ's death in the Luke version, and it is omitted from the account in St. John. I could almost wish that the *St. Matthew* had followed either course, instead of placing it directly after the crucifixion. Bach was a master symbolist, and it seems to me that his genius did not respond naturally to the realism of the text. In somewhat the same way, César Franck was invariably ill at ease when setting to music words about the wickedness of man. It is a pity that Handel did not have occasion to set the temple scene, for he, I am sure, would have portrayed it convincingly if we are to judge by his musical descriptions of natural phenomena in *Israel in Egypt*. Handel, forsooth, was capable of rending not only the veil but the whole temple singlehanded.

In Bach's B minor setting of the Mass there are plenty of opportunities for the dramatically inclined conductor. I am not thinking of the opening measures of the first "Kyrie" which, although their impact is fully in the nature of the dramatic, seem more like a declaration of the composer's fervent Protestantism—Bach, standing squarely on his two feet, admitting his sinfulness in common with all men, but seeing himself, nonetheless, as created by God in His own image and so, unwilling to take *all* the blame. There is in those measures a kind of defiant exaltation of the spiritual prerogatives of the individual which is foreign to the music of the average Roman Mass. Certainly it is found neither in the self-abasement of the Kyries of sixteenth-century Catholic composers nor in the pure theatricalism of Haydn's *Imperial Mass* or Liszt's *Missa Solemnis*.

To what a comparatively slight degree students of Bach's music have been impressed by its dramatic potentialities is evident from the infrequent appearance of the word "dramatic" in critical studies of Bach as a composer. If Bach did, at any point, infuse his music with dramatic expression, we would expect to find it first in the vocal music where its presence would be naturally invoked by the text. Unquestionably, some of Bach's secular cantatas are dramatic enough to suggest a resort to the stage.[23] But going outside the vocal field, many of the organ preludes and fantasias as well as the fugues—to take but one branch of composition—are literally textless dramas which might well challenge the art of the choreographer. Divest yourself, if you can, of the accustomed associations which gather about a performance of the great organ Passacaglia in C minor. It is a virtuoso piece and it finds a ready place on the programs of those organists who can surmount its difficulties. It is also a postlude, and its uproar has long served as a cloak for the exchange of congregational confidences. It is, besides, a temptation to the restless musical mind that cannot refrain from blowing it up to monstrous orchestral proportions. You know it as all of these, but hear it now in your mind's ear as a ballet. The somber, almost sinister, beginning; the deceptive touches of lightness; the tragedy led to its final climax through a welter of writhing, churning figures, caught without hope of salvation. I should not want to be misunderstood; I am not suggesting the transfer of this piece to the stage; I believe that the Passacaglia should stay just where Bach put it—in the literature of the organ. Nevertheless, the Passacaglia possesses, I would say, elements of the dramatic and even of the tragic.

It will not do, I think, to set the *St. Matthew* as drama against the eighteenth-century concept of drama with music. That was the opera, and in spite of sincere and often worthy demonstrations of German art, the field was largely dominated by Italian ideas and methods. It was opera in which dramatic truth struggled to make itself articulate over a preconceived and patterned form dedicated, to a great extent, to the demands of public taste. Bach never undertook the composition of an opera, but had he done so, I suspect that it would have taken the form of a *Singspiel*. His failure to enter the operatic field cannot be charged off to his devotion to sacred music, great as that was. Although accounts of his journeys would make it appear that he haunted the organ loft rather than the opera house, yet he did hear the opera at Hamburg under Keiser and in other cities as well. There is the oft-quoted remark first ascribed to Bach by Forkel, addressed to Bach's son Friedemann: "Friedemann, shan't we go again to hear the lovely Dresden ditties?" [24] But Forkel was born one year before Bach's death, so the quotation must be at least second-hand. In any case, as Bach bequeathed us no opera and no verifiable statement of his opinion of opera, we are left to deduce his dramatic convictions from music not designed for stage performance. Take the *St. Matthew* as an example: here I suspect that our tendency to pass lightly over the dramatic element arises from our proneness to view the work historically as it stands in the Passion succession, and to consider it primarily as a religious work; to see it at once as a stupendous artistic triumph and an expression of the intense devoutness of the composer. As drama it has been unfavorably compared with the *St. John*. "The *St. John Passion*," says one writer, "is on a smaller scale than its great successor and therefore less moving. But its action is swifter, and its atmosphere more tense and dramatic." [25] "The dramatic realism and conciseness of the *St. John Passion*," writes another, "contrasts conspicuously with the contemplative tone and epic composure of the *St. Matthew Passion* . . . though the latter does not lack dramatic qualities." [26] With both these opinions I venture to disagree, at the same time expressing myself as in full accord with Schweitzer who says, "The more we realize the dramatic plan of the St. Matthew Passion the more we are convinced that it is a masterpiece." [27] The next and inevitable question, then, is, could the *St. Matthew* be effectively transferred to the stage? This has been attempted, though with what success I cannot say. In 1943, Bach's *Passion According to St. Matthew* under the title "The Crucifixion of Christ— A Modern Miracle Play" was presented at the Metropolitan Opera House in New York. The leadership and artistic direction were the responsibility of a distinguished conductor; the soloists, chorus, orchestra, pantomine, and staging were, by report, of the first order. Christ was represented by a spotlight and the part of Mary Magdalene was mimed by a prominent actress. This, it seems to me, is not a type of performance calculated to make Bach's dramatic gifts articulate. The *Passion* is drama, but not melodrama, and Bach's music needs no reinforcement to heighten the tragic quality of the text. Bach's power of dramatic suggestion was infinitely subtle, and nowhere is it exhibited to such a striking degree as in the *St. Matthew Passion*.

I have long felt that this work was difficult to fit into the eighteenth-century concept of tragedy as it appears in the musico-dramatic products of that time, and an education which took the classics into some account has caused me to reflect, over the years, on the striking similarity, partly in its technique but more especially in its effect upon me, between it and certain of the Greek tragedies. I had never encountered a mention of such a possible connection in any of the literature on Bach which I had read, but I had discussed the matter with some of my colleagues and students, and not long ago one of them laid on my desk an article by D. C. Somervell entitled "The Bach Passions and Greek Tragedy."[28] In this article the author points out the correspondence in function of the various elements in the *Passion* to those in the Greek tragedy: the narrative recitative representing the episodes; and the solo arias, chorales, and devotional or meditative choruses assuming the place of the tragic chorus. I confess that the implications of all this carry me beyond Somervell's observation that there is a striking agreement between Greek tragedy and the Passion as Bach treated it; and I am sure that some, at least, must have speculated as to what was in my mind when on an earlier page I mentioned the obviously similar types of imagination possessed by Coleridge and Bach, and of the fact that the writing of a study of Bach comparable to Lowes's work on Coleridge is, at this late day, almost certainly out of the question. Is it not possible, perhaps, that Bach was actually acquainted with at least some of the works of Sophocles and Euripides? He had received a sound classical education, and he taught Latin at the *Thomasschule* in Leipzig. His Greek was, apparently, not too extensive, and it is to be assumed that he could not have read the plays in the original. Whether there existed in eighteenth-century Germany any German or Latin translations of the Greek dramatists I do not know. The problem, in any case, is to discover what classical works were in Bach's library; and this, I fear, is an almost impossible task because no inventory of that library seems to have been made during Bach's lifetime, and after his death his sons Emanuel and Friedemann divided his library, taking only that part of it which was of interest to them and leaving the rest, consisting mainly of works on theology. Without going into the various theories as to how each son's share of his father's books became dispersed, I can say that as yet I have been unable to trace any record of present ownership. The dispersion was possibly fairly wide; for example, Bach's own hymnal bearing his autograph, the gift of Emanuel to Dr. Burney, the English music historian, I came across in the Ewing Library in Glasgow.

The similarities between Bach and the authors of Greek tragedy are so many and so provocative that I shall continue, I fear, to be a nuisance to a variety of professions until I am persuaded that I have reached a dead end. Whatever significance all this may have, it may be said that it is Bach's music which transfigures the story, and it is the music that welds together all the dramatic components into an overpowering tragedy.

Here, then, is one of the puzzling contradictions in Bach's music, which presents itself again and again. It is this: how was it possible for a man who lived such a restricted life, whose whole career was so undramatic and whose music flows with such effortlessness that it seems never to have been subject to calculation—how, I say, does it come about that in his work one finds every slightest aesthetic ideal fulfilled? Without writing a single opera, his Passions and the *B minor Mass* more nearly satisfy the age-long requirements of the drama than do the out-and-out dramatic works of his contemporaries. While they were writing operas on classical subjects, requiring all the operatic panoply to be even superficially convincing, he was writing his Passions without asking any of the exteriors of dramatic presentation and was approaching much more closely than they to dramatic truth. Whatever Bach has to say is said so convincingly, with such inescapable meaning, that we may be led to believe that it cannot be said in any other way and is therefore not necessarily an emanation of genius. We do not appreciate how easy it is to be deceived by the rightness of everything in Bach until we compare him with other composers.

Enthusiasm for Handel's music is easily understandable— his speech is direct and his ideas unequivocal; but the popularity of Bach's music seems, at first thought, a little mysterious because his language is, to the lay ear, often bafflingly complex and his ideas difficult of immediate apprehension. Earlier I mentioned the long and arduous practice necessary for the performance of Bach's music. In the same way, any perception of the true inwardness of that music demands a long experience of it and close concentration on every detail.

Admittedly, this implies a discipline, but a rewarding one. In approaching the study of Bach, one is accustomed to say to students not primarily engaged in music work, "Gentlemen, you must understand that regardless of the opinion of Bach's music which you may finally come to hold, time has accorded to him a position that is not overtopped by that of any other composer; but if you are to enter into an experience of beauty which is not surpassed in any art, you will have to listen to Bach not only with your emotions but with your brains as well." Experience may warn you that the student will not relish this provision, but you are counting heavily on Bach, and you may. You are careful not to neglect mention of the emotional element, because you know that in the end, once the technicalities are taken as a matter of course, it is the emotional dynamic in Bach that will seize and hold the listener, and all except the intellectually languid will eventually come to realize that understanding, appreciation, and finally devotion come not through hearing Bach but by listening to him with every resource of mind and heart; and for your frank challenge to their intelligence they will sometime thank you. To my mind, the Bach devotees fall into three classes: first, those who, through some God-given sensitiveness, feel intuitively, and without supporting resource, the overwhelming power of Bach's music. The second class comprises what I would call the "students" of Bach. They understand the technical refinements of his style, respect the loftiness of his thought, and respond emotionally to his eloquence. It is the third class, however, that I would say comes nearest to the possession of all that springs to mind at the mention of Bach. They have—or should have—the equipment belonging to the second class, but their comprehension of Bach's total greatness is immeasurably added to by their ability to perform his music competently. All others may, happily, have much joy of Bach, but only through playing or singing him may one grasp to the full, I believe, what I have called the rightness of his art. To a certain extent, of course, an entire comprehension of what any composer is depends ultimately on a firsthand contact with his work, but out of a lifetime of experience I am convinced that this is true of Bach as it is of no other composer. Here, indeed, the organists are the most fortunate of musicians. Counterpoint seems to have been as instinctive to Bach's musical expression as everyday speech is to us, and the organ was the predestined and ideal instrument for contrapuntal writing—the organ with its several keyboards and manifold registers permitting each line to achieve its full destiny; with its pedal board, adding both feet to the performer's resource; and above all with its range of volume which made possible all dynamic gradations from the softest to that demanded by the majesty of the fugue at its climax. It is only necessary to consider the large number of Bach's organ works and their variety to be persuaded that this instrument was the natural outlet for his inspiration and the most normal conveyance of his ideas. As in so many other details connected with this composer, one thinks of Albert Schweitzer and of his reverent and self-effacing performance of the organ works. My first acquaintance with this came many years ago in Paris, when, as a student, I sang in the chorus of the Bach Society. There, time after time, with one eye on my score and the other on the conductor, but with both ears keenly attentive to the organ, I marveled at the utter propriety of Schweitzer's realizations of the continuo parts. The criticism of his interpretation of Bach's major organ works is that it is colorless; that he plays only the notes; but what more, one may in all conscience ask, is necessary? The adulteration of Bach's pure and finite eloquence by the addition of "readings" calculated to make the music "effective" approaches close to artistic sacrilege. Possessing a thorough knowledge of the organ of Bach's time and of the traditions of organ playing under which Bach composed, Schweitzer, through his straightforward, unadorned, and impersonal performance, almost persuades one that it is Bach himself who is playing.[29] I would say that of all men living, Albert Schweitzer stands nearest to the truth.

If I seem to have stressed the eminence of Bach to the apparent neglect of Handel, I apologize, and I hasten to reaffirm the latter's importance; for as I said at the very beginning the consummation of baroque music was made possible only through the contributions of both men. It remained for Handel to teach the Italians what the Italian type of opera could be in the hands of a really great composer, and to leave the oratorio in its completed and perfected form, at the same time filling it with such impressive choruses that probably every composer from that day to this has studied his works in an effort to discover the secret of his power. It remained for Bach to leave the fugue, the cantata, the chorale prelude, and the Passion at a point beyond which they never advanced; and both men dealt so eloquently with types like the suite, sonata, and concerto of their time that they are looked upon as the ultimate expressions of those forms. Indeed, they wrought so conclusively with certain techniques and styles of composition that the road to future development in those directions was closed, and whether willingly or not their successors had no other recourse than to strike out on new paths.

Little if any of Bach's life bears material relation to his

music. His genius was all-embracing and seems quite apart from Bach as an individual. Perhaps it is the sublimity of his music that sometimes seems to stand between us and him. One feels that there was no limit to his imagination or to the varied quality of his eloquence. Sometimes his music sounds like routine thorough-bass music, sometimes it sounds romantic, sometimes modern; but it is always Bach; and when he withdraws into himself as he so often did, especially in his chorale preludes, so profound and poignant is his musical speech that there is no other eloquence like it.

If not much of Bach's life is to be read into his music, the case with Handel is quite different. Every note of his choruses, in particular, is autobiographical. Examples of the recording in his music of the exteriors of a composer's existence and of what we believe to be his nature are not numerous. Beethoven is certainly one, for his music bears witness not only to the elements of his character as evidenced in his behavior, but also to the physical changes he underwent, such as his increasing deafness. Palestrina, whose life would appear to have been a model of piety, displays even in his secular music a restraint which stands in marked contrast to the intensely colorful and worldly expression of many of his Italian colleagues. Gesualdo, living at the same time, endowed his music with every device of secular appeal and seems occasionally to have transferred to his choral pieces a personal preoccupation which has made him quite famous apart from his music; for Gesualdo, in addition to being a composer and a prince of Venosa, was an expert poisoner, and this lethal habit, according to the singers who have withered under the vocal difficulties he contrived, is clearly exercised in his music. Bruckner's calm seems to be lived over again in a sometimes too convincing fashion in his symphonies. Berlioz's music is a vivid confirmation of his temperament and his beliefs, for his career no less than his compositions speaks loudly of his devotion to romantic ideals. Of these composers, Beethoven appears as the clearest example of personality and music combined in one expression, but Beethoven's character was infinitely complex and one may justly believe that there was a good deal of Beethoven that never found its way into his music. Handel's character, on the other hand, was relatively uncomplicated, and everything that he was, as far as we know him, is steadily reflected in his musical output. He is the prime example of a composer whose music is literally himself.

Bach was a man of strong will and high principle, and these are laudable virtues, but genius that he was, one feels that he would have written equally great music had he been a weakling. Handel was proud, arrogant, despotic, but above all courageous. He was forever being opposed by forces which were theoretically stronger than he was; several times bankruptcy engulfed him; he suffered two strokes of paralysis and went blind; yet none of these afflictions deterred him in the slightest. If you wish to call the genius of Bach all-embracing or even cosmic, then the genius of Handel is clearly of this world, but it is of the kingdoms of this world; it is grand, spacious, majestic.

The distinction which is usually made between the music of these two men is that Bach's is objective while Handel's is subjective, and this, on the whole, is a true distinction, for Bach seems to have written without any effort to make an obvious record of his emotions, and certainly with only slight consideration for exterior circumstance. One of the few occasions when Bach paid attention to the practical aspects of composition was in his church cantatas. The performance of a cantata was accorded thirty minutes of the time devoted to

67

the service, and G. W. Woodworth has pointed out that if you time any one of the church cantatas of Bach you will find that it lasts just one half hour. Handel, however, was the most practical of men. The opera, the most spectacular and gainful form of the day, one which Bach entirely eschewed, was Handel's particular love. He yearned to be a success as an opera composer, and when one compares his scores with those of his contemporaries, one is persuaded that though his failure resulted from a diversity of causes, one major reason for it was the fact that he simply could not squeeze the towering bulk of his genius within the confines of so stilted a form as the serious opera of his time. Handel's true destiny was fulfilled in the oratorio, a field in which he has never had a rival.

If Bach composed mainly for his own edification and the glory of God, Handel wrote for the public; and by the same token it takes much more concentrated listening to get at the heart of Bach's music than it does to fathom Handel's. There is a passage in the *Collected Mathematical Papers of James Joseph Sylvester* which seems to me to represent, in actual experience, just this difference. This is the passage:

"As an artist delights in recalling the particular time and atmospheric effects under which he has composed a favourite sketch, so I hope to be excused putting upon record that it was in listening to one of the magnificent choruses in the 'Israel in Egypt,' that, unsought and unsolicited, like a ray of light, silently stole into my mind the idea (simple but previously unperceived) of the equivalence of the Sturmian residues to the denominator series formed by the reverse convergents. The idea was just what was wanting,—the key-note to the due and perfect evolution of the theory." [30]

Now Sylvester may have solved his problem while listening to Handel, but had he been listening to Bach, without any doubt whatever either Bach or the problem would have come off distinctly second best.

Although Bach was a relatively late discovery, his music, nonetheless, has had a prodigious influence from the nineteenth century to our time, and his contrapuntal skill still serves as the inevitable and unattainable model for students of composition. Withal, he is a composer probably heard today more often than any other, and the most "popular" in the highest sense of that word. Handel's influence has been uninterrupted, and the roster of composers who have been his devotees is impressive. One thinks of Haydn, then an established composer, hearing *Messiah* probably for the first time and, overwhelmed by its choral brilliance, profiting by his experience to the immeasurable benefit of the *Creation* and *The Seasons;* of Schubert coming on the scores of Handel's oratorios in the last year of his tragically short life, engaging a teacher to guide his contrapuntal studies, and dying before his intention could be realized.

Both Bach and Handel preserved their musical vitality to the end of their lives. The *Triumph of Time and Truth*, Handel's last oratorio, is even more alive than the early *Utrecht Te Deum;* and in Bach there is a crescendo of power from the music of his youth to the chorale prelude *When We Are in Deepest Need*, his valedictory work, dictated, because he was blind, to his son-in-law. James Munn once observed to me that in literature a similar unflagging vitality is found only in Homer and Dante, and without attempting to find a literary parallel to the music of Bach, he suggested that Handel's magnificent style is comparable to that found in the works of Dryden. He further commented on the presence in the later music of Bach of an element that is found in the last plays of Shakespeare, and which he described as the conversion of a primary impulse into a "vast placidity."

Try if you will to find these qualities in their music, or to identify the sources upon which they built their great edifices; analyze their technical methods and estimate their eloquence in terms of the comparatively restricted musical language of their day. Do all this, and in the end you return to the music itself in its wholeness, the final and irrefutable evidence of their greatness.

APPENDIX
AND NOTES

Appendix

The illustrations accompanying the lectures were performed by Michel Parlier, violinist; by the Mary Baldwin College Choir; by members of the University of Virginia Orchestra conducted by James Berdahl; and by members of the University of Virginia Glee Club.

"Behold the Lamb of God," from *Messiah*, by George Frederick Handel

"Then Round About the Starry Throne," from *Samson*, by George Frederick Handel

"Fecit potentiam in bracchio suo," from the *Magnificat*, by Johann Sebastian Bach

Largo–Allegro, from the *Concerto Grosso in C minor*, opus 6, number 3, by Arcangelo Corelli

Allegro, from the *Concerto Grosso in F major*, opus 6, number 9, by George Frederick Handel

Allegro, from the *Brandenburg Concerto Number 1, in F major*, by Johann Sebastian Bach

Preludio, from the *Sonata in E major* for unaccompanied violin, by Johann Sebastian Bach

Adagio, from the *Sonata in E major* for violin and clavier, by Johann Sebastian Bach

Notes

1. Ernest Newman, "Bach and Handel, the Historical Perspective," the *Sunday Times*, London, February 19, 1939.

2. Albert Schweitzer, *J. S. Bach*, translated by Ernest Newman, 2 vols. (London: A. & C. Black, Ltd., 1923; New York: The Macmillan Co.), I, 230. Used with permission of The Macmillan Company.

3. J. A. Fuller Maitland, *The Age of Bach and Handel* (London: Humphrey Milford, Oxford University Press, 1931), vol. IV, The Oxford History of Music, p. 40.

4. Hugo Leichtentritt, *Music, History, and Ideas* (Cambridge: Harvard University Press, 1938), p. 143ff.

5. Charles Sanford Terry, *Bach's Orchestra* (London: Humphrey Milford, Oxford University Press, 1932), p. 24.

6. Schweitzer, *J. S. Bach*, II, 297.

7. Schweitzer, II, 299f.

8. W. G. Whittaker, *Fugitive Notes on Certain Cantatas and the Motets of J. S. Bach* (London: Humphrey Milford, Oxford University Press, 1924), p. 220.

9. C. S. Terry, *The Music of Bach: An Introduction* (London: Humphrey Milford, Oxford University Press, 1933), p. 86.

10. C. Hubert H. Parry, *John Sebastian Bach: The Story of the Development of a Great Personality* (New York and London: G. P. Putnam's Sons, The Knickerbocker Press, 1909), p. 223.

11. I remember that some years ago when the Harvard Glee Club and the Radcliffe Choral Society were preparing the *Magnificat* for performance with Dr. Koussevitzky and the Boston Symphony Orchestra, one of the singers told me—and I confess that I was not surprised—that in the early hours of the morning he had encountered a group of Glee Club members staggering across Boston Common singing in perfect canon and with confident though bibulous piety, "Omnes, omnes, omnes, omnes generationes."

12. C. S. Terry, *Bach: The Historical Approach* (London and New York: Oxford University Press, 1930), p. 14.

13. *The Bach Reader: A Life of John Sebastian Bach in Letters and Documents*, edited by Hans T. David and Arthur Mendel (New York: W. W. Norton & Co., 1945), p. 26.

14. Schweitzer, I, 196.

15. For a scholarly and impartial consideration of this matter see Sedley Taylor, *The Indebtedness of Handel to Works by Other Composers* (Cambridge: At the University Press, 1906).

16. The entire autograph manuscript of *Jeptha* is reproduced in the Handel *Gesellschaft*, Vol. 97. The particular page referred to is to be found in Newman Flower, *George Frederic Handel: His Personality and His Times* (Boston and New York: Houghton Mifflin Co., 1923), opposite p. 320. On p. 320 there is a translation of Handel's two notes.

17. John F. Runciman, *Old Scores and New Readings . . Discussions on Music & Certain Musicians* (London: At the Sign of the Unicorn, MDCCCCI), pp. 61–63.

18. Karl Young, *The Drama of the Medieval Church*, 2 vols. (Oxford: At the Clarendon Press, 1933), I, 80.

19. Young, I, 110.

20. Young, I, 492.

21. Michael Tippett, *A Child of Our Time: An Oratorio* (London: Schott & Co. Ltd., 1944), Schott ed. 10065.

22. Donald F. Tovey, *Essays in Musical Analysis*, 6 vols. (London: Oxford University Press, 1937), V, 34.

23. A few years ago I witnessed a dramatically convincing presentation of the *Coffee Cantata*, sung and acted by amateurs. I recall one delightful innovation contributed to the occasion by the entire audience's adjourning to the foyer to enjoy coffee, cream, and sugar, all generously provided by a wholesale coffee company.

24. "Friedemann, wollen wir nicht die schönen Dresdener Liederchen einmal wieder hören?" J. N. Forkel, *Über Johann Sebastian Bach's Leben, Kunst und Kunstwerke* (Leipzig: Hoffmeister und Kuhnel, 1802), p. 48: The translation given is on p. 335 of the *Bach Reader*.

25. Terry, *Music of Bach*, p. 75.

26. Manfred F. Bukofzer, *Music in the Baroque Era from Monteverdi to Bach* (New York: W. W. Norton & Co., 1947), p. 295.

27. Schweitzer, II, 210.

28. D. C. Somervell, "The Bach Passions and Greek Tragedy," *Music and Letters*, Vol. 27, No. 4 (October, 1946).

29. An expansion of this idea may be found in the author's article, "The Transcendentalism of Albert Schweitzer," *The Albert Schweitzer Jubilee Book*, edited by A. A. Roback (Cambridge: Sci-Art Publishers, 1945).

30. *The Collected Mathematical Papers of James Joseph Sylvester*, I (Cambridge, England: At the University Press, 1904), 616.